Copyright © 2018 by Wendy J Hall

All rights reserved.

Cover and Illustrations by Ysha Morco.

No part of this book may be reproduced in any form or by any electronic or mechanical means including information storage and retrieval systems, without permission in writing from the author. The only exception is by a reviewer, who may quote short excerpts in a review.

This book is a work of fiction. Names, characters, places, and incidents are based on input from professionals, research by the author and fictitious details.

Wendy J Hall
Visit the website at
https://www.mediwonderland.com/

First Printing: September 2018
Mediwonderland

ISBN-13: 978-1727303957

DEDICATION

To all of my trach patients throughout the world, thank you for teaching me how to be chronically ill with strength, pizzazz, grace and as a self-advocate. You rock, Lisa!

Tracy's Tracheostomy

Wendy J. Hall

Tracy is seven years old. When she was a baby, the doctors found she had a very narrow windpipe but it was mild and she didn't need treatment.

However, one day, she complained to her mom that she had a hard time breathing. They took her to see Dr. Daniel.

Dr. Daniel examined Tracy carefully and ordered some scans. Then he said her subglottic stenosis had worsened and that she would need a tracheostomy.

"A trachy what?" Tracy asked.

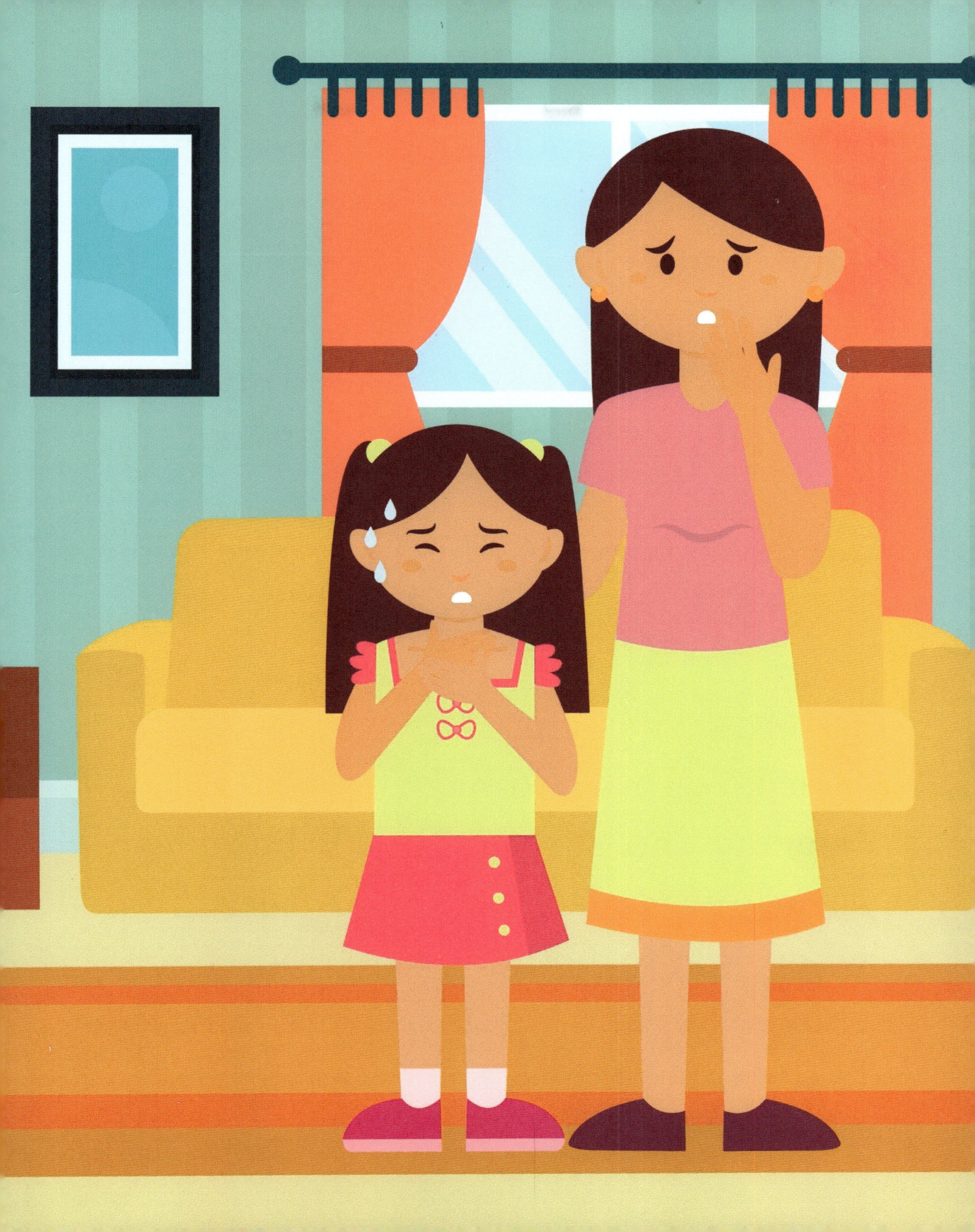

"A tracheostomy is a procedure where we make a hole in your windpipe so the air enters easily. Your windpipe is too narrow for you to breathe properly and not enough air is getting into your lungs and that is dangerous."

Tracy wanted to run away and hide because she was scared.

"There's nothing to worry about, Tracy," Dr. Daniel said calmly. "During the surgery, you'll be asleep so you won't feel a thing. Afterwards, when you're better, Nurse Nina will show you and your parents how to take care of it at home."

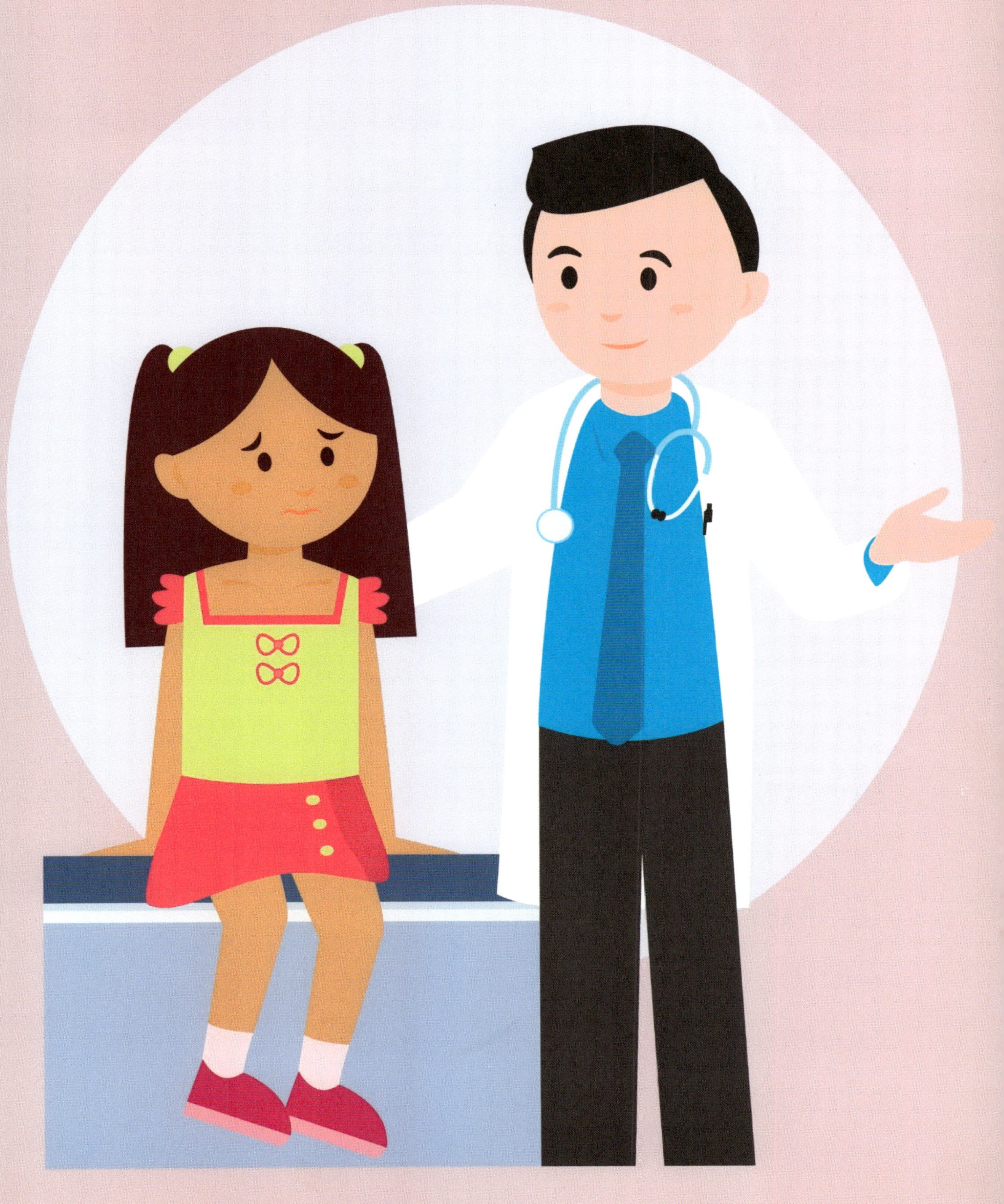

Her mom said she could choose some special pajamas and she could take her iPad to watch movies and read stories. She chose pajamas with kittens on them.

Two days later, Tracy went to the hospital, feeling very nervous.

"Hi, Tracy!" said Dr. Daniel, when she was settled in her bed, reading Mediwonderland stories.

"Before we prepare you for surgery, I want to show you something." Dr. Daniel showed her a white bent tube with straps attached to both sides.

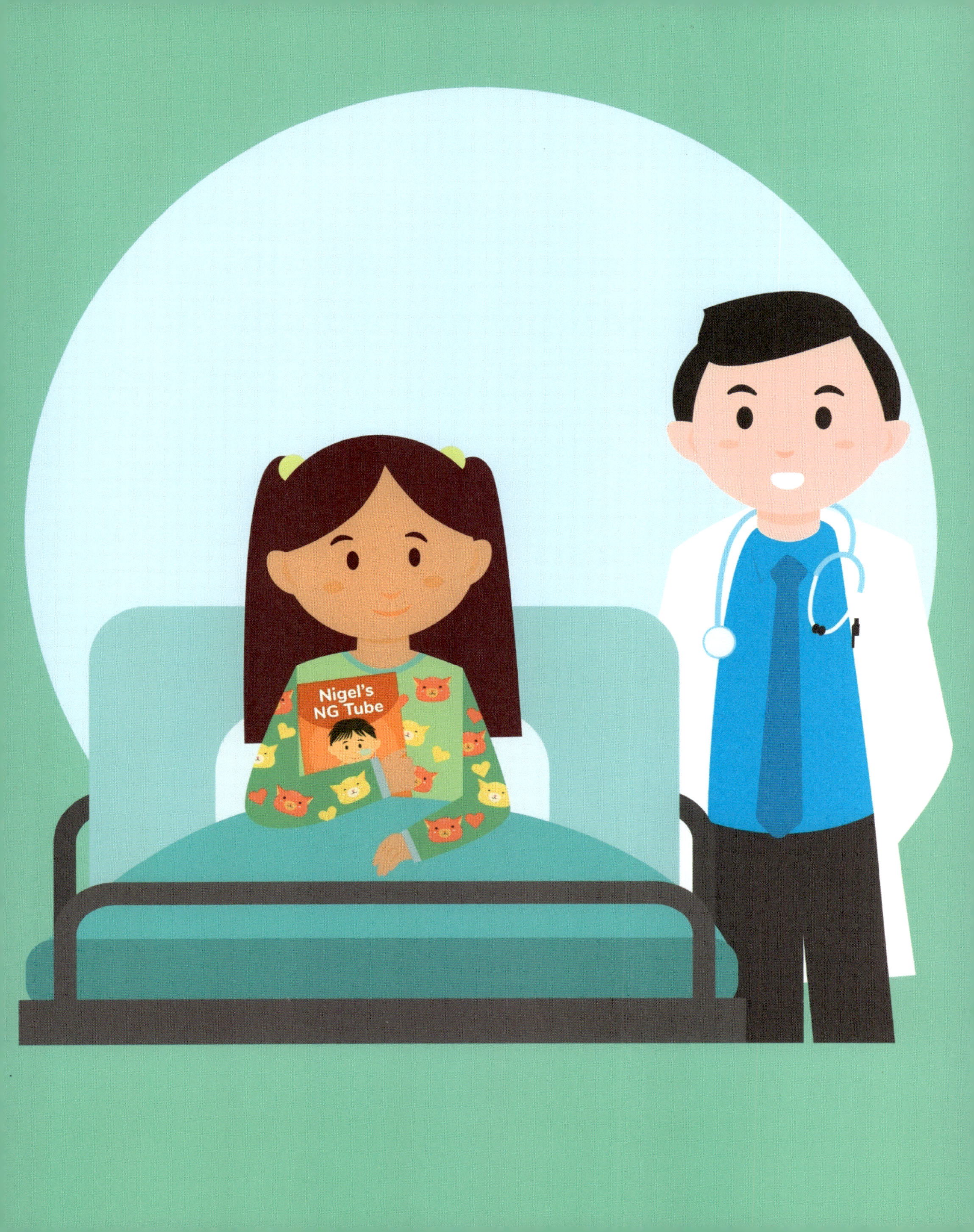
Nigel's
NG Tube

"This is a tracheostomy tube," Dr. Daniel said, "Or 'trach tube' for short. After we make a hole in your windpipe, we'll put this into the hole. You'll breathe through it and it'll make you feel much better!"

"Is that like a second nose?"

Dr. Daniel laughed. "That's right, Tracy."

"That's cool!" Tracy kissed her parents and was taken into a room with lots of equipment and a big light. The nurses were kind to her and said she was very brave.

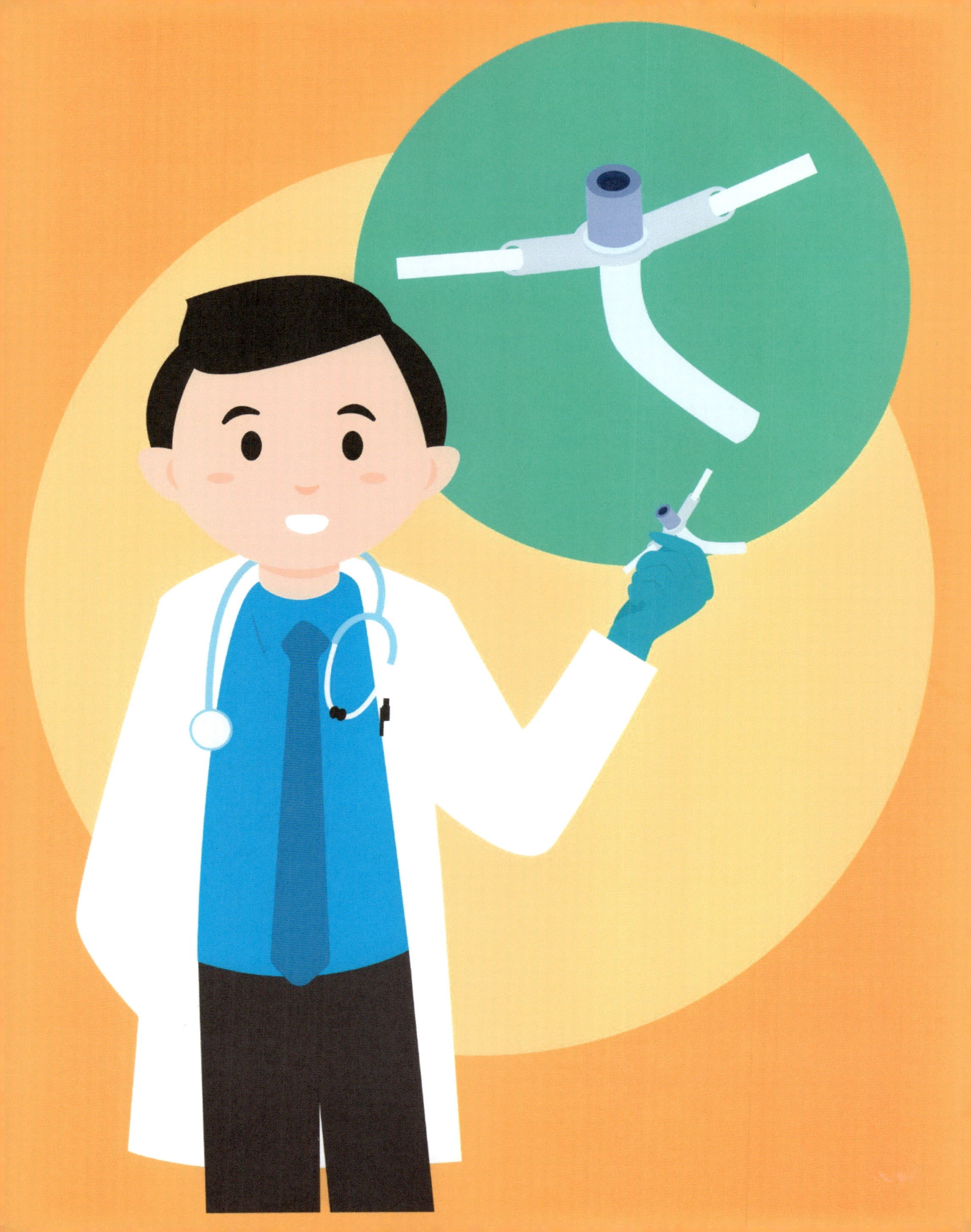

One of them put a mask over her mouth and then asked her to count to ten.

The next thing she knew, her mom, dad and Dr. Daniel were standing beside her bed.

"How are you feeling, sweetheart?" Tracy's mom asked.

"I feel okay," Tracy said. "But my throat feels weird… My voice sounds different too!"

"That's normal after a tracheostomy. Would you like to take a look in the mirror?" Dr. Daniel asked.

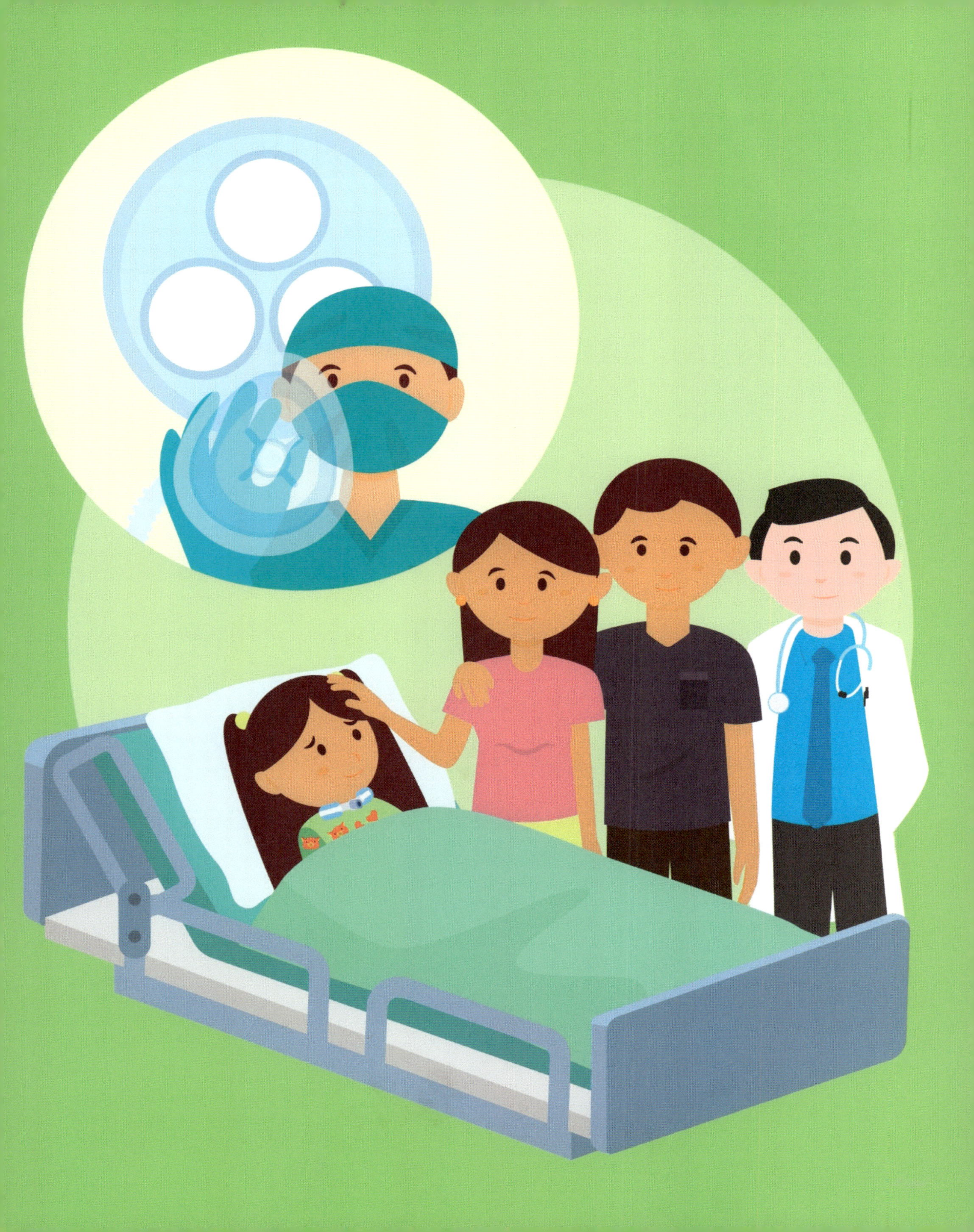

Dr. Daniel handed Tracy a mirror.

Tracy looked at her neck. "It looks a bit like a big necklace," she said.

"Yes it does," said Dr. Daniel. "For the first few days, you'll feel a bit of pain and you'll have your food through the tube in your nose. Once it's healed, you can eat again."

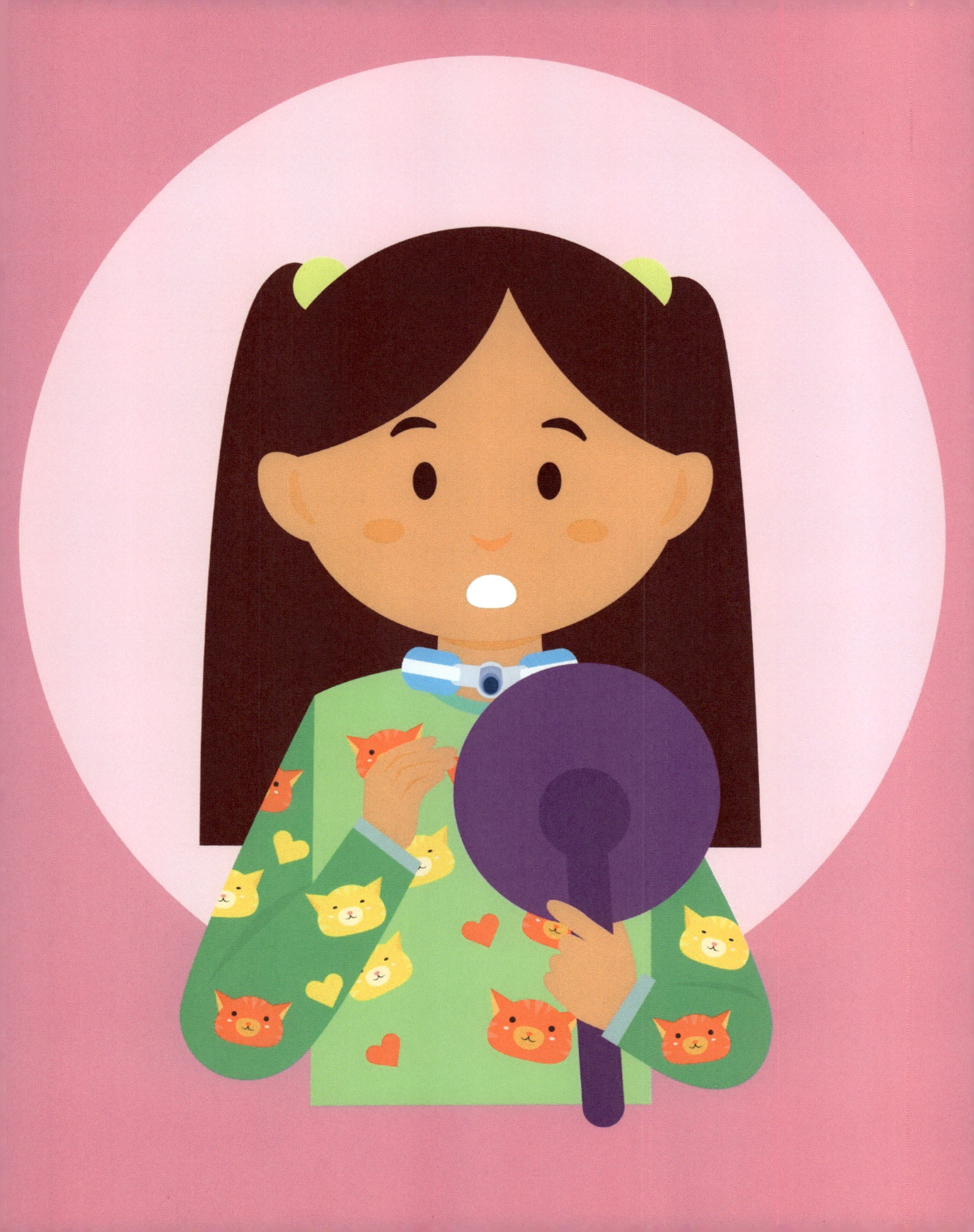

Tracy stayed in the hospital for a week.

Every day, Nurse Nina came to care for her trach whilst her mom watched, reading through the "Tracheostomy Care" booklet she had been given.

After a week, Tracy felt much better and Dr. Daniel said she could go home.

TRACHEOSTOMY CARE KIT

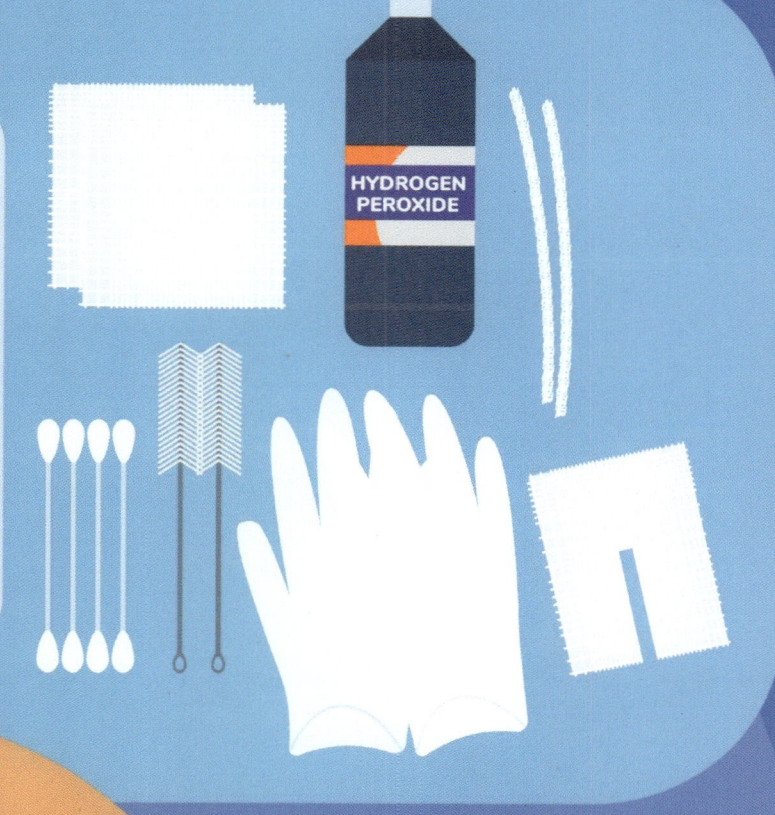

HYDROGEN PEROXIDE

Tracheostomy Care

"Because you're such a brave girl, you get to wear a special badge. The badge said 'Junior Trach Club' on it."

"You'll need this," said Dr. Daniel. "In fact, you'll need it tomorrow for a special meeting."

Tracy was curious.

After thanking Dr. Daniel, Tracy went home with her parents and a lot of equipment.

"I'm so proud of you, sweetheart," Tracy's mom said with a hug.

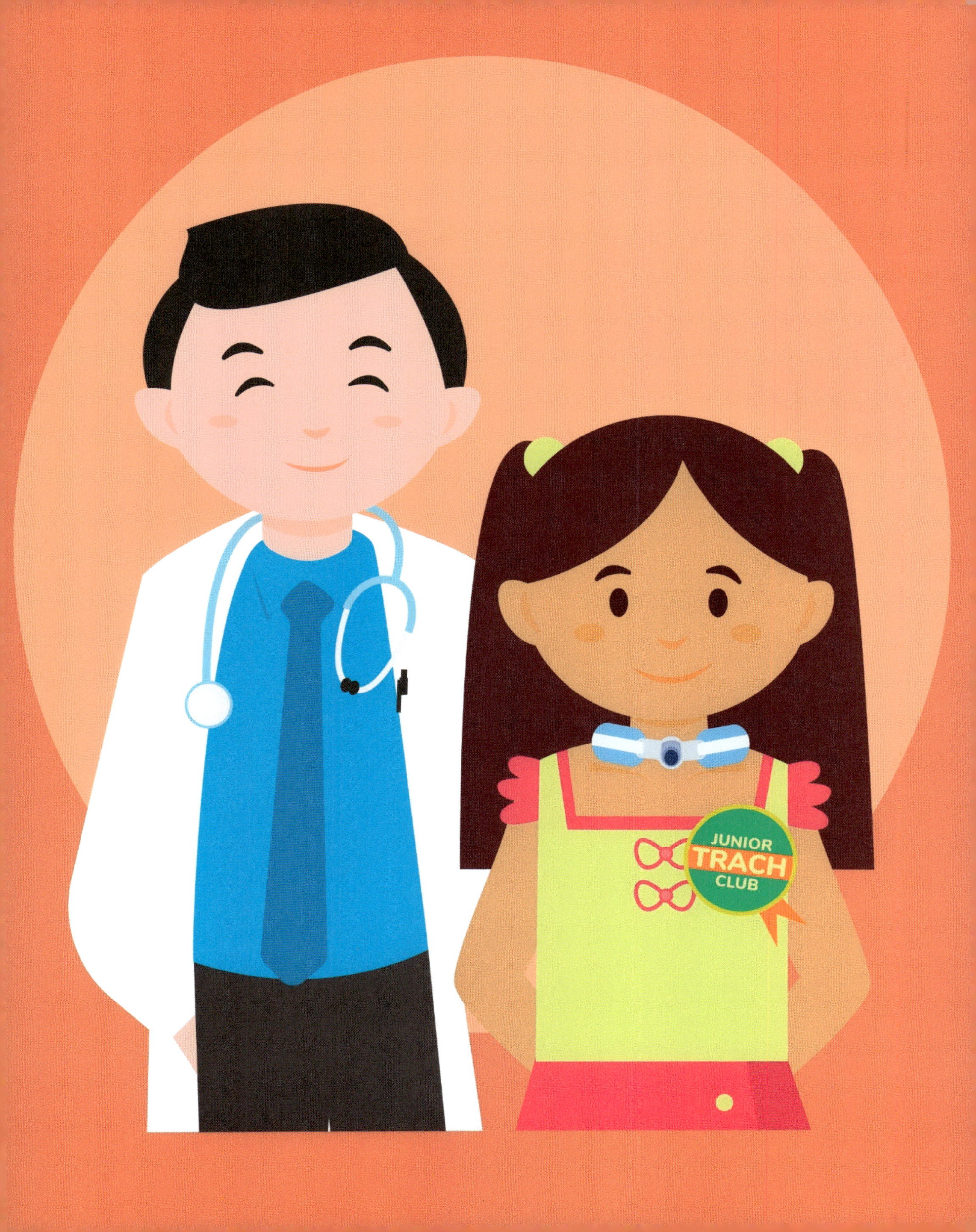
JUNIOR
TRACH
CLUB

The next day, Tracy's mom and dad took her to a center where there were kids sitting in a circle and parents sitting in chairs at the back. To Tracy's surprise, the kids all had trachs, just like she did!

A therapist named Miss Annie welcomed her and invited her to sit down.

"Everyone, I'd like you to meet Tracy, our newest member. Today, after introducing yourselves, we're going to learn more about home care. Tracy, why don't you go first?"

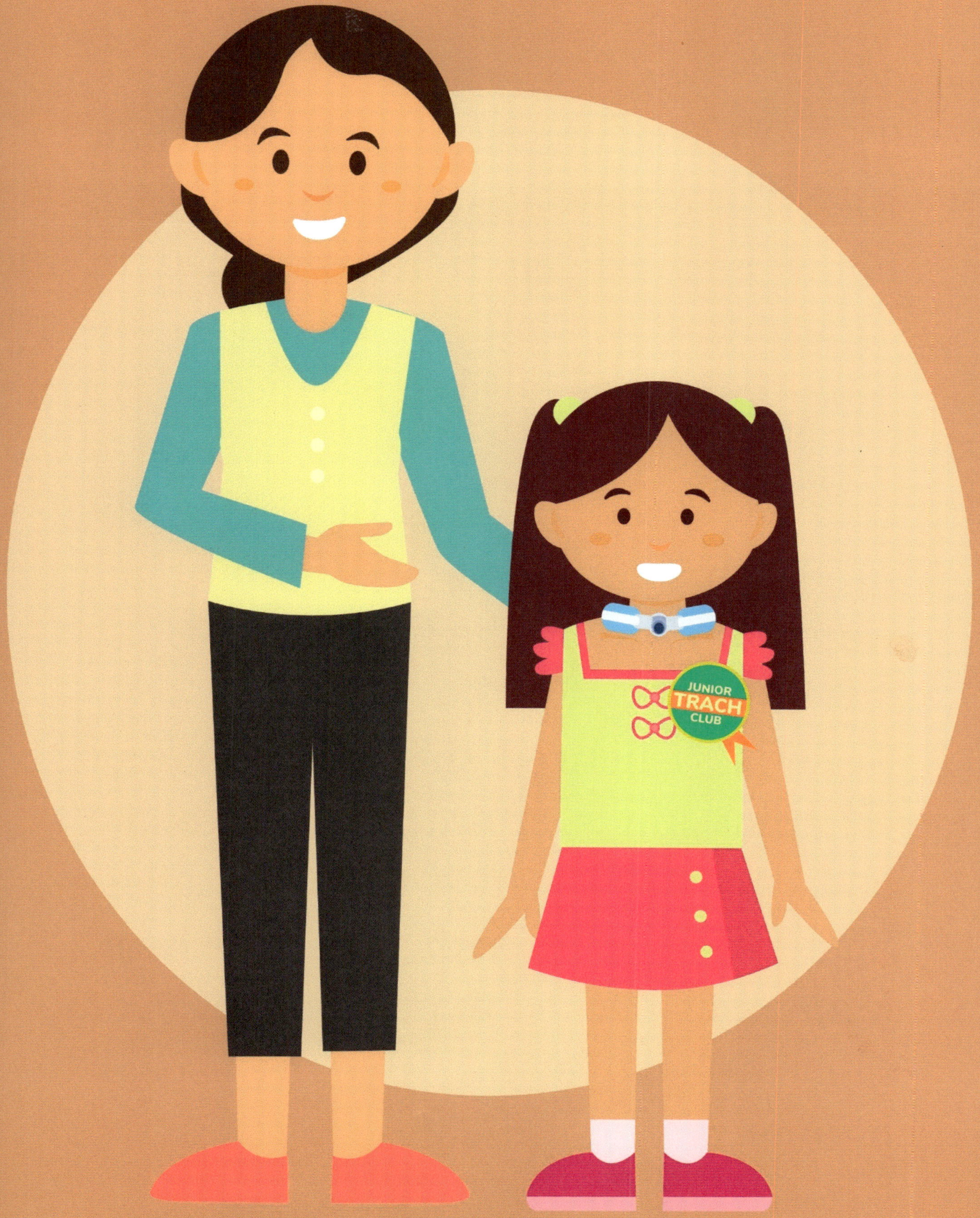
JUNIOR
TRACH
CLUB

Tracy shared her experience and then the other children talked about theirs. Some had oxygen tubes attached to their trachs and some of the conditions were hard to pronounce.

One boy didn't have a trach. He only needed one when he was young, but wanted to stay in the Club!

Tracy also noticed that the kids had different kinds of trach tubes. Some had ones that opened from the sides. Some had tubes with caps on them. Many kids needed to put a finger over their tubes to be able to speak normally.

JUNIOR TRACH CLUB
JUNIOR TRACH CLUB
JUNIOR TRACH CLUB
JUNIOR TRACH CLUB

Then Miss Annie said, "Now it's time for us to play a game. I've written the steps for home care on some cards. You'll separate into two teams, A and B." Tracy was in Team A.

"You have to put the cards on the wall in the right order, so you need to work together.

Ready, get set, go!" The children rushed to put the cards on the wall.

Once they had finished, Miss Annie looked at the cards on the wall and announced, "Congratulations Team A! You are the winning team." Everyone clapped. "Let's go through the cards."

- Care for the tracheostomy ~~
- Change the tube and suction.
- Check for signs of infection and get medical help if needed.
- Wipe outward from the stoma.

JUNIOR TRACH CLUB

"Some of you will have different instructions from your doctors and your parents will follow those."

1. Care for the tracheostomy twice a day.
2. Wash your hands thoroughly and use sterile gloves if necessary.
3. Change the tube and suction.
4. Clean the stoma.
5. Check for signs of infection and get medical help if needed.
6. Use a cotton swab dipped into sterile water or saline.
7. Wipe outward from the stoma.
8. Dry the skin with swabs or gauze.
9. Use a dressing if necessary.

1. Care for the tracheostomy twice a day.
2. Wash your hands thoroughly and use sterile gloves if necessary.
3. Change the tube and suction.
4. Clean the stoma.
5. Check for signs of infection and get medical help if needed.
6. Use a cotton swab dipped into sterile water or saline.
7. Wipe outward from the stoma.
8. Dry the skin with swabs or gauze.
9. Use a dressing if necessary.

After that, they had a tea party.

Tracy was happy because she made a lot of friends who were just like her. She couldn't wait to see them again at their next meeting.

She knew that being a trach kid was going to be a big challenge, but she also knew that she was not alone.

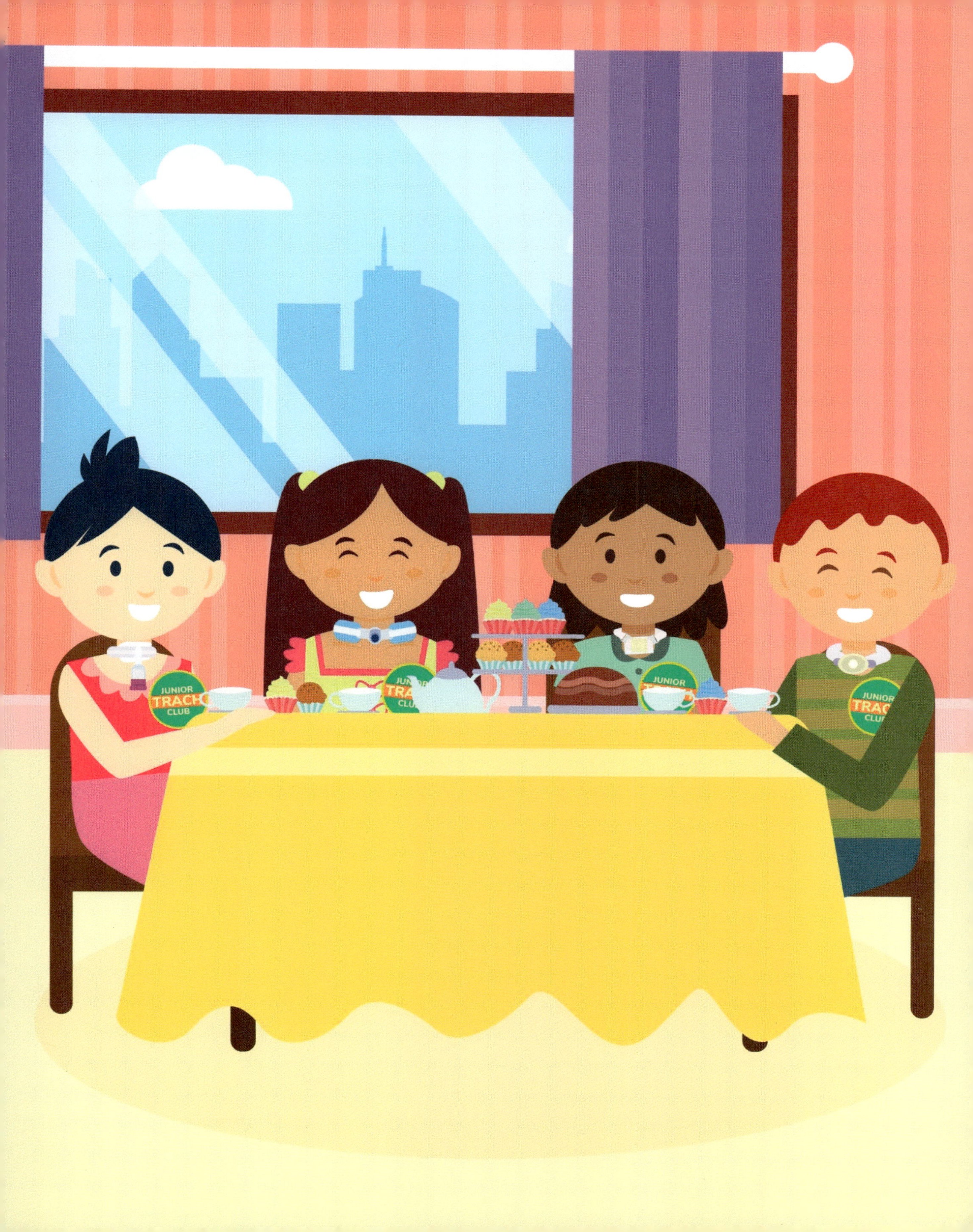
JUNIOR
TRACH
CLUB

About the Author

Originally from the UK, Wendy speaks five languages and has authored over 100 educational books. The inspiration for this innovative series comes from personal experience: Her own daughter, then aged eight, once spent a year in hospital and underwent major surgery.

While taking care of a scared child, Wendy could not find materials that helped her navigate the healthcare system. This situation kindled a dream: to provide parents and medical professionals with a tool to make medical procedures, illnesses, and adverse childhood circumstances less frightening.

Wendy has extensive knowledge of the medical field as she herself suffers from a rare, chronic illness. An award-winning Patient Leader, she works to improve healthcare by advocating and educating.

To learn more about Wendy, please visit the website:

https://www.mediwonderland.com

Printed in Great Britain
by Amazon